m·i·n·d·g·a·m·e·s

Network Games

by Ivan Moscovich

A network, or graph, is any arrangement of points, interconnected by lines or edges, in a plane or a three-dimensional space.

Our world is filled with networks. We travel on networks of roads, we click on a channel of a TV network to watch our favorite programs, and we use e-mail or surf the Web on the Internet, a computer network that links smaller networks around the world.

Take the Network challenge and tackle the fascinating puzzles in this book. I guarantee you'll have fun!

IVAN

illustrated by
David Brion

Workman Publishing · New York

Sir Hamilton: A Tribute

Sir William Rowan Hamilton, born in 1805 in Dublin, Ireland, is regarded as one of the greatest mathematicians in the English-speaking world. A child prodigy, he learned to read English by the age of three; Latin, Greek, and Hebrew by age five; and Arabic and Sanskrit by the time he was ten.

He was a brilliant student at Trinity College in Dublin and became Astronomer Royal of Ireland at the age of twenty-two.

But mathematics, especially number theory and calculus, remained his passion.

At a meeting of the British Association for the Advancement of Science in 1857, Hamilton presented a puzzle that involved tracing a path around the 30 edges, or sides, of a dodecahedron (a solid figure with 12 pentagonal faces). This was the inspiration for "Put a Spin on It," which is a tribute to his genius.

Put a Spin on It

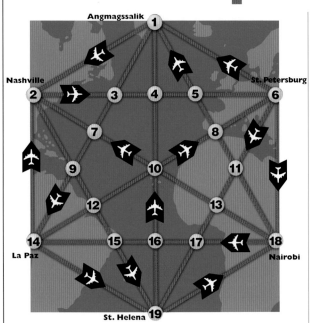

For 1 Player

Captain Hamilton, owner of All-Around Airways, really likes games. That's why his airline offers a unique tour package, and it's a doozy—six cities, no more, no less. What's more, the captain likes to change the itinerary for each tour by spinning the arrows on his flight planner. To make things even *more* interesting, the captain will give you a free trip if you can figure out a single path for the plane to follow after he spins the arrows.

Your challenge

● Using the gameboard on the cover, match the configuration of arrows shown at left. Then create a single, direct path, following the direction of the arrows, through each of the six destinations, and visiting each city only once.

How to play

❶ Use the point of your pencil to trace a path from city to city, following the direction of the arrows, *without* retracing any lines.

❷ Write down the names or numbers of the six cities in the order they can be visited.

(answers on page 20)

Fickle Flight Control

For 2 or More Players

Invite two or more friends to play the Fickle Flight Control game.

Your challenge

● Using the gameboard on the cover, find the number of single paths that can be created, following the direction of the arrows.

How to play

❶ Player One spins the arrows so that they end up in a random configuration facing in either direction along one line.

❷ Player Two writes down the names or numbers of the six cities in the order that they can be visited by looking at the gameboard. Player One then tries to find an alternate path for the same configuration, writing down the names or numbers of the cities in a different order that they can be visited. Players take turns until no new routes can be found for this configuration of arrows.

❸ Now, play another round. This time Player Two sets up the board by spinning the arrows, and Player One tries to find a single path connecting the six cities, writing down the names or numbers in the order that they can be visited.

❹ Again, take turns until no more paths can be found. The player who ends up with the greatest number of single paths wins the game.

extra challenge: To create a continuous path connecting each of the 19 numbered intersections on the gameboard, using the same configuration of arrows as in "Put a Spin on It." This time you can turn to another line when you come to an intersection, but you can visit each intersection only once. The player who creates the *longest* path, connecting the greatest number of intersections, is the winner. Set a time limit of five minutes for each player.
(answer on page 20)

REMEMBER: You must always move along a line in the direction of the arrow.

The Königsberg Walk

For I Player

There once was a town along the Pregel River in East Prussia named Königsberg. (It's still there, only now it's the city of Kaliningrad, it's in western Russia, and the river is called the Pregalya.)

The town has seven bridges that cross different branches of the river. The people of Königsberg were fond of taking walks. But they wondered if they could go for a stroll, crossing each bridge only once, and end up where they started.

Your challenge

● To figure out why it's not possible to cross each bridge only once and return to where you started.

How to play

❶ First analyze the problem by breaking it into simpler walks, using only one or two bridges. What do you conclude?

❷ Would the Königsberg walk be possible if you added or took away one bridge?
(answers on page 20)

●The Mad Maze of Dr. M

For I Player

The a-mazing Dr. Mensa has created a maddening maze. Once you're in it, there's only one way out. Do you dare to begin?

Your challenge

● To draw a single line that passes through the entire maze, connecting all the points *without* retracing any lines.

How to play

❶ Trace the maze on a piece of paper or photocopy it from the book.

❷ Without taking your pencil off the paper, and without leaving the white outlines, trace a line through all the red points. You may revisit any point, but you may not retrace a line.

(answer on pages 20–21)

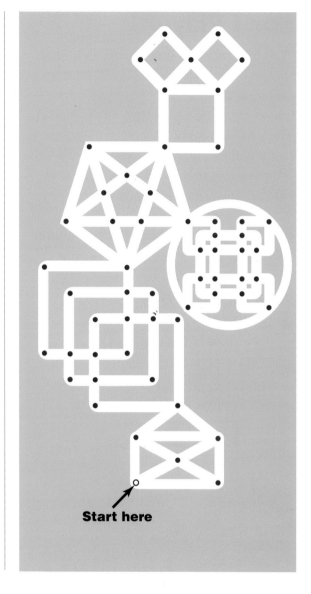

Start here

hint: Look at each distinct shape in the maze and see what happens if you apply Euler's Rule, as explained in the answer section on page 20, "The Königsberg Walk." According to to Euler, a path exists through a maze if there are no more than two points with an odd number of lines coming out of them.

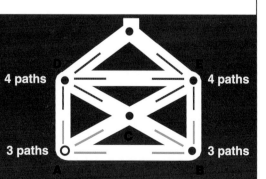

4 paths — D ... E — 4 paths

3 paths — A ... C ... B — 3 paths

●Party Puzzler

For I Player

"You have no idea how hard it is to plan the perfect party," sighs Diana, who is planning a Sweet 16. "You have to mix guests up perfectly so that not everybody who's invited knows everybody else, or the party will be an absolute dud. That's why I always like to make seating plans before I throw one of my excellent parties."

Can you figure out the secret to Diana's success?

Your challenge

● In a party of you and your friends, any two of you are either mutual friends or mutual strangers. Can you invite four or five friends to your party, avoiding groups of three who are all mutual strangers or mutual friends?

● friends   ● strangers

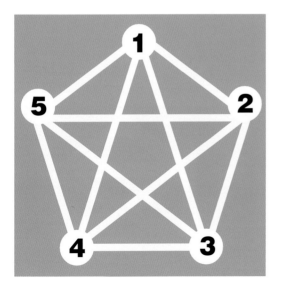

How to play

❶ Trace the figures on paper or photocopy them from the book. The numbers represent the people at the party.

❷ Using a red and a blue pencil, connect the lines between the numbers in the five-point figure so that none of the triangles is made up of three red lines or three blue lines.

❸ Now play the game using the six-point figure. What answer do you get?
(answers on page 21)

In the 1920s Frank Ramsey stated that "complete disorder is an impossibility." Any structure will always contain an orderly substructure. Structural Ramsey Theory illustrates how complex a structure must be to guarantee a certain substructure by proving how many numbers guarantee a certain pattern. His theory is crucial in designing better communication and transportation networks.

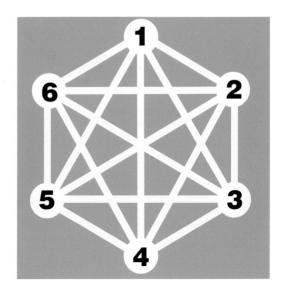

●Cave Save

For I Player

Five unhappy tourists are lost in an underground cave with many chambers. Their guide is outside, waiting to pick them up, but he doesn't know where each person is. He knows there are red and blue arrows painted on the floor of the cave, so he calls out a sequence of red arrows and blue arrows for them to follow, which will lead to the center chamber, where he will meet them.

Your challenge

● To work out the sequence of red arrows and blue arrows that will lead each tourist to the center chamber. *(answer on page 21)*

> **hint:** Each tourist must follow exactly six arrows. Some tourists may enter the center chamber more than once during the sequence.

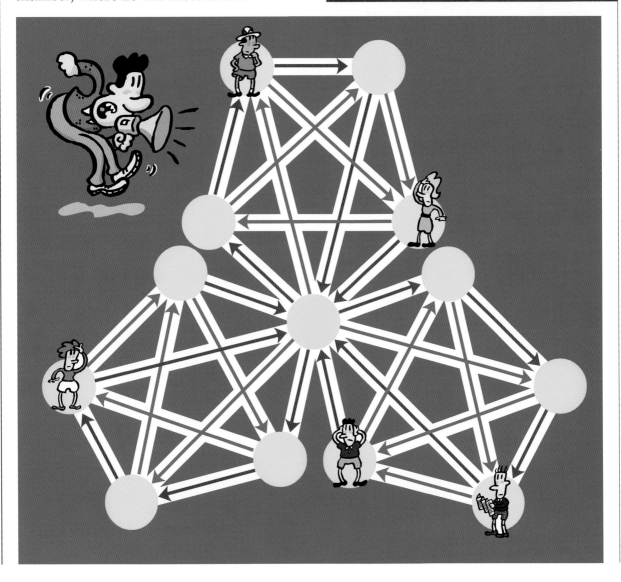

●Mole City

For 2 Players

Once there were some little moles
Busy digging little holes.
To keep from getting all confused
They had a system that they used.
Each mole would mark its exit spots
With two nice, matching colored dots.
There was a law in this mole town
For tunneling beneath the ground.
Their paths could be quite indirect
But they could never intersect.
As long as those paths never crossed
The little moles would not get lost.

Your challenge

● To connect pairs of same-color dots within the white grid lines without creating any intersections.

How to play

❶ There are three different games at the right. You can make your own gameboards by tracing these samples or by taking graph paper and drawing in the dots with colored crayons, as shown at right.

❷ Taking turns, each player must trace a line that connects two same-color dots.

❸ The first player unable to connect the dots without intersecting any lines loses the game.

FOR MATH WHIZZES ONLY!

extra challenge: For one player, to connect every same-color dot in each puzzle, without intersecting any lines.

(answers on page 21)

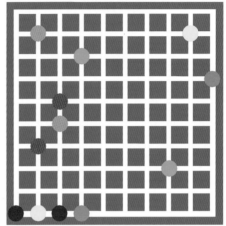

GAME 1

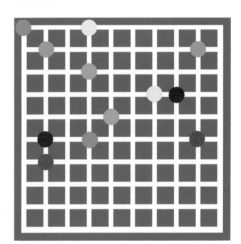

GAME 2

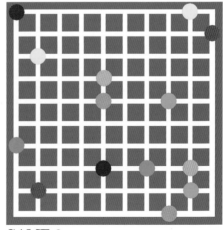

GAME 3

●Floor Story

For I Player

The Queen of Spumonia is having a floor installed in the Great Hall. She just fired the last royal floor person, and you're the new one. You must complete the pattern in each row, but first you have to figure out what it is. The queen is known for her bad temper, so you want to get it right.

Your challenge

● To figure out the shape that belongs in each of the empty squares in each row.
(answer on page 22)

●Off with Your Heads!

For I Player

Now the queen wants to change the floor pattern in the royal bathrooms. But she wants it done in a very special way.

Your challenge

● To figure out the fewest number of moves it will take to transform the figures at left into the figures at right.

How to play

❶ Only complete rows (horizontal) or columns (vertical) can be switched or reoriented.

❷ A move consists of switching any two rows or columns, or reorienting one row or one column.
(answers on page 22)

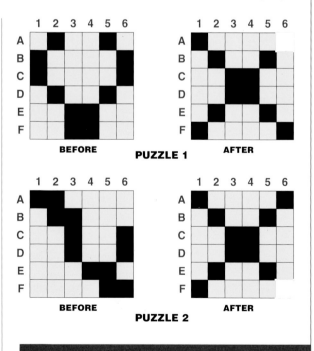

hint: You can create your own strips of squares to solve the puzzle.

I Was Framed!

For 1 Player

You're at an outdoor art show when you happen to meet the creator of an amazing sculpture called *Nest of Frames*.

"Which frame is the biggest?" you ask the artist.

"That's for you to figure out," he replies.

You say to yourself, "If the red frame fits over the blue frame and blue frame fits over the yellow frame, then wouldn't the yellow frame be smallest? But then again, the yellow frame fits over the red one. What's the story?"

Your challenge

● To figure out how the sizes of the frames are related to one another.

How to play

● The best way to figure this out is to make three frames yourself. Take a piece of flexible cardboard and use a ruler to measure and cut out three rectangular frames of exactly the same size. (It's even easier if you have three pieces of cardboard that are the same size to begin with!) Now try the same thing, but with three square frames. What do you conclude?

(answer on page 22)

Raiders of Lost Cubes

For I Player

The once-beautiful 5 x 5 x 5-foot multi-colored cube has been vandalized. This dastardly act was the work of the Cubettes, a devilish band of math-whiz cube thieves, who made off with lots of the smaller cubes. The more colored sides there are on a cube, the more valuable it is. So this gang got quite a haul.

Insurance Inspector Widget is on his way. But before he arrives, you want to assess the damage yourself.

Your challenge

● To figure out how many of each kind of cube are missing, assuming the bottom surface of the cube has no color.

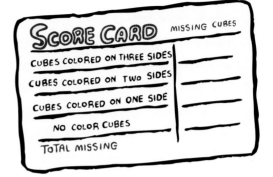

How to play

● Begin by making a score card and filling in the blanks. Then add up the numbers to get your total.
(answer on page 22)

hint: There is a visual shortcut that can help you count the missing cubes and check your results. Can you figure it out? Does it help if you stand on your head?

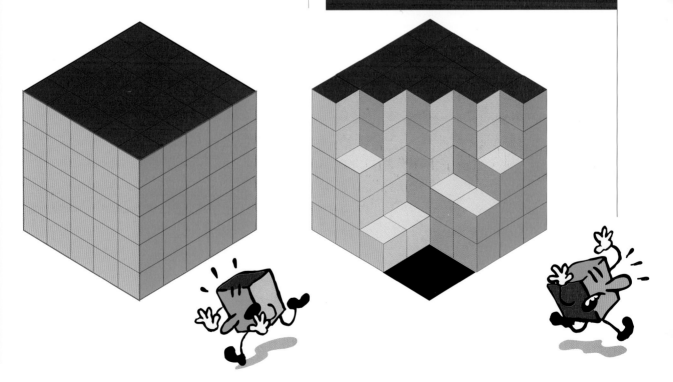

●A Stirring Problem

For I Player

Oops! It's a bad day at the Rainbow Café. Somebody just dropped a bunch of colored coffee stirrers on the floor. They've fallen in a pile, and all but one is either flat on the floor or parallel with it. Which of the colored stirrers has fallen on an angle?

hint: Begin at the bottom of the pile, and work your way to the top.

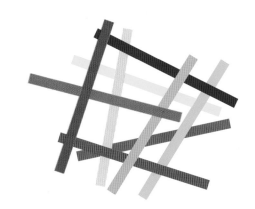

Your challenge

● Looking down from the top, to figure out which stirrer is at an angle.
(answer on pages 22–23)

●Seeing Stars

For I Player

You can create your very own constellation in the shape of a convex pentagon from a field of nine randomly placed stars. When you finish, you can name it after yourself—like Kenopia or Ursula Major.

If you can create more than one constellation, you can name it after a friend.

Your challenge

● To connect five of the nine stars to form a convex pentagon—one without any broken inside angles.
(answer on page 23)

Ramsey Theory (page 6) was redefined by Paul Erdös in the 1930s, with the introduction of problems like this one.

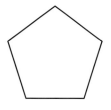

CONVEX PENTAGON

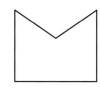

CONCAVE PENTAGON

Knot or Not

For I Player

Spike and Lady are involved in a dispute over a piece of rope. Lady thinks the rope is hers since one end of it is in her yard. Spike thinks it's his since the other end is in his yard.

It's not even a nice piece of rope. It's messy and tangled, but they don't care about that. It's fun to growl. Because they're dogs, they don't know that there are going to be knots in the rope when they're done pulling it straight. But since you have a human brain, you can figure out which tangles will form knots and which ones will not.

Your challenge

● To figure out which tangles of rope will form knots and which ones will slip through when the rope is pulled tight. *(answer on page 23)*

hint: In order to form a knot, a piece of string or rope must have at least three crossings—over, under, and over itself—that cannot be rearranged so that there are no crossings. You can test each section of this puzzle with a piece of string.

●Good Knight!

For 1 or 2 Players

In the game of chess, a knight may go to any square that is distant one square horizontally and two vertically or two squares horizontally and one vertically.

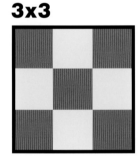

To play the game, you can trace the game-boards or draw your own on graph paper.

note: In your answer to the uncrossed knight's tour, the knight's path must be indicated by a straight line from the space where the knight begins to the space where he lands after he makes a legal move. The answer on a 3 x 3 board appears at far left.

5x5

4x4

3x3

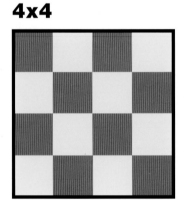

7x7

6x6

Challenge 1

● To create an uncrossed knight's tour, meaning that the knight does not cross his earlier path. Try this on all five remaining gameboards. How far can you get?

How to play

❶ Start on any square on each gameboard with the objective of creating an uncrossed knight's tour.

❷ For two players, Player One starts on any square on the 8 x 8 gameboard. Players take turns continuing the uncrossed knight's tour from the last position reached.

❸ The winner is the last player able to make a move.

One of the oldest math problems, dating back to the 1700s, is called the Crossed Knight's Tour. It asks: Can the knight be made to visit every square of the board exactly once by making a series of legal chess moves?

Challenge 2

● To create a crossed knight's tour, meaning that the knight may cross any square multiple times, but must land on each square only once. Try on all gameboards. *(answers on page 23)*

hint: If you know about graphs, you can think of this as a graph problem, with intersections, or nodes. In knight's tours, you join the nodes according to the rules of the game.

8x8

Take a Rook at This

For I Player

Unlike the knight, the rook (or castle) can move either horizontally or vertically as far as it likes. In this game, however, it can visit each square of the gameboard only once.

Challenge I

● To determine the least—and the most—moves that the rook can make in a tour under the following conditions. Begin the rook's tour at the top left-hand corner of the board and move to the last yellow square on the bottom right, using the fewest possible moves. Now try again. What is the maximum number of moves a rook can make?

Challenge 2

● To connect the top left-hand corner square with the top right-hand corner square in the minimum number of moves. Now try again: What is the maximum number of moves a rook can make?

extra challenge: Begin anywhere on the board and complete an uncrossed closed rook's tour by passing through every square on the board only once. A closed tour means the rook must return to its original square.
(answers on page 24)

The Bishop's Tour

For I Player

In chess, a bishop can only move diagonally and on a single color on the board. If a bishop starts on a green square, it can only move to another green square, as far as it wishes, but only in a straight line.

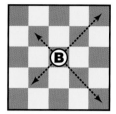

bishop can visit by moving diagonally and not visiting any square more than once.

hint: It's impossible to visit all the green squares.

Challenge I

● Starting on the second green square from the left in the bottom row, to figure out the maximum number of squares the

Challenge 2

● Starting on the green square at the top left, to make a bishop's tour that includes visiting every green square on the board. You're allowed to revisit some squares, but the idea is to visit as few as possible.

(answers on page 24)

The Winner's Circle

For I Player

Selma Smart of Einstein High has come up with a new kind of Tic Tac Toe game.

Your challenge

To place three circles—one red, one yellow, one blue—in each row and each column. One row and one column are filled in. Now, can you complete the rest?

note: Four circles in each row and each column will remain empty.

(answer on page 24)

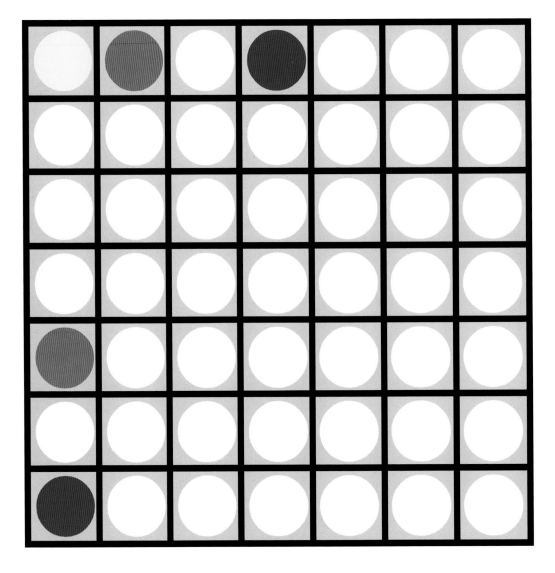

●Petunia's Pickle

For I Player

Poor Princess Petunia. As repayment for a loan of twenty bucks, a mean little guy has locked her up in a tower until she figures out how to solve this puzzle. "Can't I just guess your name?" the princess wails. "That's the usual thing."

"No way," he replies. "I won't let you out if you can't solve this puzzle."

Your challenge

● To transfer the three coins from the left side to the right side so that they end up in the same order in mirror position: the biggest at the bottom and the smallest at the top.

How to play

❶ Take a nickel, a penny, and a dime, and place them on the gameboard.

❷ Slide one coin at a time from one channel to another, never leaving the white area. Never jump over another coin and never place a coin on a circle smaller than itself. (A coin can move across circles smaller than itself as long as the circles are empty.) What is the minimum number of moves you can make?

(answer on page 24)

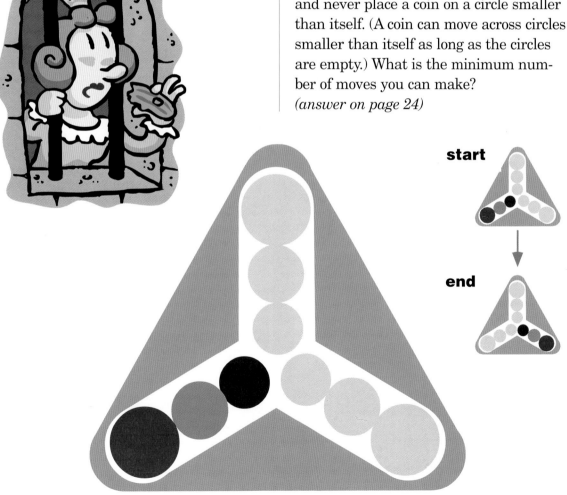

start

end

ANSWERS

page 2 PUT A SPIN ON IT

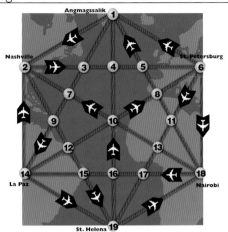

There is more than one possible answer to the puzzle. One answer is: London - Los Angeles - New York - Paris - Sydney - Tokyo, or 1 - 14 - 2 - 6 - 19 - 18.

Another is: London - New York - Paris - Tokyo - Los Angeles - Sydney, or 1 - 2 - 6 - 18 - 14 - 19.

It's amazing but true that no matter how the arrows are placed after each spin, there is always at least one single path interconnecting the six cities.

page 3 FICKLE FLIGHT CONTROL

Extra challenge: Using the exact same configuration of arrows as shown above, one possible solution to the puzzle is: 8 - 6 - 18 - 11 - 13 - 17 - 19 - 16 - 10 - 4 - 5 - 1 - 2 - 3 - 7 - 9 - 14 - 12 - 15. Can you find others?

page 4 THE KÖNIGSBERG WALK

Leonhard Euler, the famous Swiss mathematician, was able to figure out the conditions in which such problems are solvable.

First, he created a diagram showing the relationship between the four pieces of land and the seven bridges. Each piece of land is indicated with a letter (A, B, C, D), and each bridge with a number (1, 2, 3, 4, 5, 6, 7).

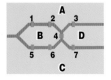

Euler determined that since you can cross each bridge only once, each time you cross a bridge, you must have another bridge to bring you back. Therefore, there must be an even number of bridges leading to and from each piece of land. If any area on the diagram has an odd number of bridges, the walk cannot be completed.

Now look at section A. There are three bridges from A: 1, 2, 3. Look at section B. There are five bridges: 1, 2, 4, 5, 6. Then look at sections C and D. There are three bridges from each: 5, 6, 7 and 3, 4, 7. Obviously, it is *not* possible to complete this walk and return to the place where you started.

Euler also determined that, if you are not concerned with getting back to where you started, but just want to cross each bridge once, you can complete the walk as long as you don't have more than two pieces of land with an odd number of bridges.

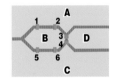 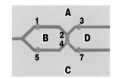

"The Königsberg Walk" is possible if you move bridge 3 to connect B and D and eliminate bridge 7. Another possible answer is to move bridge 2 to connect B and D and eliminate bridge 6. In either case, there is an even number of bridges connecting the pieces of land.

The solution Euler created works not only for "The Königsberg Walk," but for any maze problem.

page 5 THE MAD MAZE OF DR. M

As shown in "The Königsberg Walk," Euler came up with a rule that will enable you to solve any tracing puzzle of this kind, without resorting to the time-consuming trial-and-error method.

To solve the maze, check how many paths are going in or out from every intersection marked with a red point.

In a maze as complicated as this one, take each section independently. First, look at the bottom section. There are three possible paths from A and B and four from C, D, E, and F. We now know it is possible to pass through every section of this maze, but it will *not* be possible to return to the starting place.

Now do the same for each of the other sections. You will determine that every other point has an even number of paths, so the maze can be completed.

It is important where you start the puzzle. The solution for starting at the bottom left-hand corner of the maze is shown below. You could also start at the bottom right-hand corner and complete the maze.

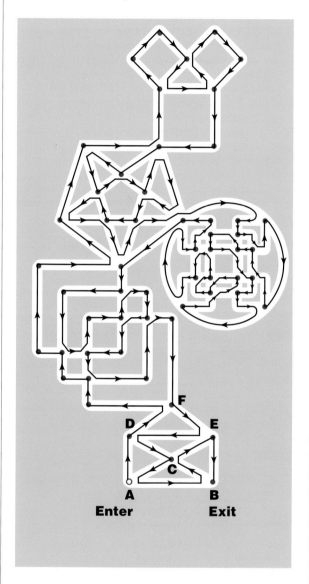

A
Enter

B
Exit

You may pass through the same red point coming and going. The arrows indicate the direction of the path. There is only one possible path.

page 6 **PARTY PUZZLER**

In a group of five, you can avoid having any group of three be all friends or all strangers. But you can't avoid this in a group of six. No matter how you color the graph, you will be forced to close a red or blue triangle at the last line, if not before.

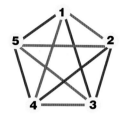

page 7 **CAVE SAVE**

The sequence of instructions given to the lost tourists is: R - B - B - B - B - R. This will lead the five lost tourists to the middle cave.

page 8 **MOLE CITY**

Extra challenge for one player: One solution to each of the three games, without any lines intersecting, is shown below:

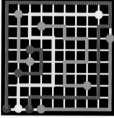

GAME 1

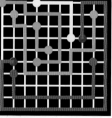

GAME 2

GAME 3

page 9 FLOOR STORY

In each row the yellow parts (fractions of unit squares) must add up to exactly one unit square. Here's one way to solve it:

page 9 OFF WITH YOUR HEADS!

The fewest number of moves in Puzzle 1 is three.

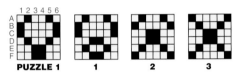

1. Switch D and E.
2. Switch C and F.
3. Switch A and B.

The fewest number of moves in Puzzle 2 is six.

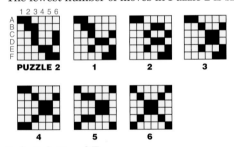

1. Switch D and E.
2. Reorient B.
3. Switch B and C.
4. Reorient F.
5. Switch 2 and 6.
6. Switch 3 and 5.

page 10 I WAS FRAMED!

The three frames in the *Nest of Frames* sculpture are identical and can be arranged in any way. These frames are rectangular in shape, and it will be necessary to slit one side of one of the three frames to create this figure. It will not work with square frames.

page 11 RAIDERS OF LOST CUBES

There are 5 small cubes in each row, so each outer side of the large cube has 25 smaller cubes (5 x 5), and the total number of small cubes is 125 (5 x 5 x 5).

Beginning at the bottom level of the cube as shown in the puzzle, you are missing 4 cubes: 1 is not colored, 1 is blue, 1 is green, and 1 is blue/green. Moving up to the second row, you are missing 6 cubes: 2 are blue, 1 is blue/green, 2 are not colored, and 1 is green. On the third level, you are missing 8 cubes: 2 are blue, 1 is blue/green, 2 are green, and 3 have no color. On the fourth level, you are missing 10 cubes: 3 are blue, 3 are green, 1 is blue/green, and 3 have no color. The top row is also missing 10 cubes: 3 are red/green, 3 are blue/red, 3 are red, and 1 (the corner cube) is all three colors.

For a shortcut, turn the cube upside down. The missing cubes will appear as solid cubes, which makes them easier to count!

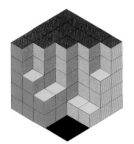 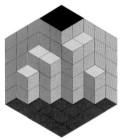

Right side up   Upside down

SCORE CARD	MISSING CUBES
CUBES COLORED ON THREE SIDES	1
CUBES COLORED ON TWO SIDES	10
CUBES COLORED ON ONE SIDE	18
NO COLOR CUBES	9
TOTAL MISSING	38

page 12 A STIRRING PROBLEM

The dark green stirrer is the only one at an angle.

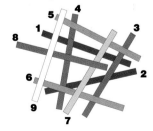

Starting from the bottom up, stirrers 1 and 2 are resting on the floor. Next come 3 and 4; and 5 and 6. The next level has just one stirrer, 7. Stirrer 8 is at an angle since one end is resting on stirrer 7, but the other end is resting on the floor. Stirrer 9 is the topmost one in the pile, and it is parallel to the floor.

page 12 SEEING STARS

It has been proven that nine points will *always* create a convex pentagon in any configuration of nine randomly placed points. One convex pentagon is shown above.

page 13 KNOT OR NOT

To see which configurations lead to knots, picture pulling on each end of the rope. You will see that no knot will form in figures 1, 2, 3. But in figure 4, the rope loops over and under itself, and a knot will form when you pull the rope straight.

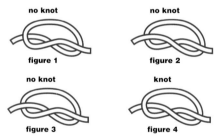

The two middle loops (3 and 4) will become knots; the rest will slip through.

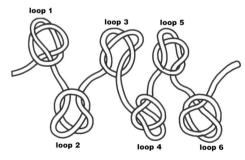

page 14 GOOD KNIGHT!

Uncrossed Knight's Tour

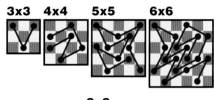

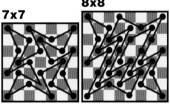

Note that on this 7 x 7 board the uncrossed tour is closed, meaning that the knight returns to his original square after the final move.

Crossed Knight's Tour

Beginning with 1, the squares are numbered to indicate the knight's progress.

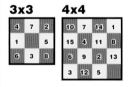

Note that a crossed tour is impossible to complete on the 3 x 3 and 4 x 4 boards.

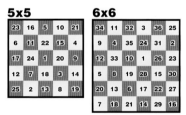

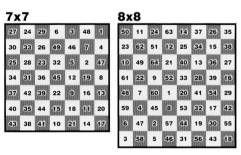

The total number of crossed knight's tours on the 7 x 7 board is over 6,000, while the number of knight's tours on an 8 x 8 board is nearly 82,000. Note that on the 6 x 6 and the 8 x 8 boards, the crossed tours are closed.

page 16 **TAKE A ROOK AT THIS**

Challenge 1: Starting at the top left-hand corner of the board and moving to the last yellow square on the bottom right, the fewest moves you can make is 21; the most moves you can make is 55.

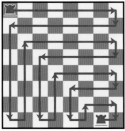
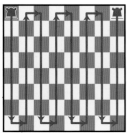

**minimal solution
21 moves**

**maximal solution
55 moves**

Challenge 2: Connecting the top left-hand corner with the top right-hand corner, the fewest moves you can make is 15; the most moves you can make is 57.

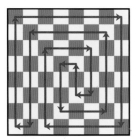
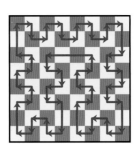

**minimal solution
15 moves**

**maximal solution
57 moves**

Extra Challenge: No matter where you begin on the board, you can complete a closed tour in a minimum of 16 moves moving horizontally, and a maximum of 56 moves if you go through each square.

**minimal solution
16 moves**

**maximal solution
56 moves**

page 17 **THE BISHOP'S TOUR**

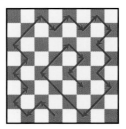

Challenge 1: The best that can be achieved in a bishop's tour when squares are not allowed to be revisited is 29 green squares. No matter how the bishop moves, there will always be at least three unvisited green squares.

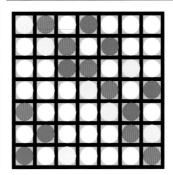

Challenge 2: If we allow the bishop to revisit squares, it is possible to visit every green square. Starting at one corner and ending in the opposite corner, this can be done in a tour of 17 moves.

page 18 **THE WINNER'S CIRCLE**

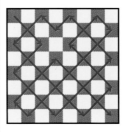

Here is one solution. Answers may vary.

page 19 **PETUNIA'S PICKLE**

Only seven moves are needed to transfer the three coins, as shown below. The red represents a quarter; the green, a nickel; and the blue a dime.

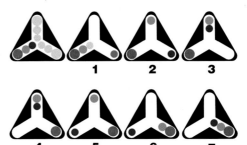